The Life and of William Shakespeare

Written by Sue Purkiss

Illustrated by Giorgio Bacchin

Contents

Collins

Prologue

In 1588, England was facing a terrible threat.
In the ports across the English Channel, the Spanish
Armada had gathered. This was a great fleet of
warships – and its purpose was to attack England.
For many years now, the English and the Spanish
had been enemies. It was partly to do with religion.
Fifty years before, the king of England was Henry VIII.
At that time, England, like all the other countries of
Europe, was Roman Catholic. The head of the church
was the Pope in Rome. But for a number of reasons,
Henry fell out with the Pope. He decided to start his
own religion. So now England became Protestant, and
everyone had to belong to the Church of England –
the head of which was Henry.

unmanned English ships set on fire and filled with explosives to blow up among Spanish ships

A lot of Catholics, including Henry's daughter, Mary, were unhappy about this. When she became queen, she said England must turn Catholic again, and she even married Philip, the Catholic king of Spain. By now, most of the English had settled into being Protestants, so this made Mary very unpopular. When she died in 1558, her younger sister Elizabeth became queen. Elizabeth was young, clever, beautiful – and Protestant. Most people loved her, and England cheered up.

Elizabeth I

Elizabeth didn't really mind whether people were Protestant or Catholic. But the Catholics did mind, and they plotted to get rid of her and put a Catholic ruler – Elizabeth's cousin, Mary Queen of Scots – on the throne instead. King Philip, back in Spain, did all he could to help them. This went on for years, but eventually, in 1587, Elizabeth's advisers persuaded her that she had no choice; Mary must be **condemned** to death. Philip was furious.

Spain also had another problem with England. English ships kept attacking Spanish ones and stealing treasure from them – treasure that the Spanish had in turn stolen from people they had conquered, particularly in South America. So Philip was angry about that, too.

Everyone was very worried when news came that the Armada was ready to attack. But the English ships were small and fast, and their captains were cool and clever. Under the skilful leadership of Sir Francis Drake, they ran rings round the big, unwieldy Spanish ships. Also, the English had a great stroke of luck – a terrible storm rose up and drove the battered Armada north round the coast of Scotland.

Sir Francis Drake seizing Spanish ships

But the danger wasn't over. The Spanish army, gathered across the Channel in Dunkirk, could still invade.

The Battle of Gravelines near Dunkirk. The English ships were firing to prevent the French escaping along the shore.

5

The English army met at Tilbury in Essex.
It wasn't a full-time army. Many of the soldiers were inexperienced and afraid. How would they cope if the Spanish invaded? Elizabeth knew she must do something to inspire them – she had to make them believe they could win.

So, she put on a white dress and a breastplate made of silver. Then, sitting on a white horse, she rode out to Tilbury to meet them – and made the speech of her life. This is part of it.

"I know I have but the body of a weak and feeble woman; but I have the heart of a king, and of a king of England too; and I think it foul scorn that Parma or Spain, or any prince of Europe, should dare to invade the borders of my realms ..."

The message was clear. If a woman could be so brave and **defiant**, how could they fail to be the same?
But Elizabeth wasn't the only one who had
an impressive way with words. A young man had
recently arrived in London from his home town of
Stratford-upon-Avon. So far, no one had heard of him.
But one day he'd be even more famous than Elizabeth;
his name would be known all over the world.
He was called William Shakespeare.

Elizabeth makes her speech to the troops at Tilbury

Stratford-upon-Avon

In the April of 1564, a baby boy was born to John
Shakespeare and his wife Mary in Stratford-upon-Avon,
a market town with timbered houses and a river
with swans. They'd already lost two other babies – both
girls – so this child must have been extra precious.
They called him William.

John's father had been a farmer, but John was
a glover. It was a highly skilled trade: the gloves he
made for the aristocracy were exquisite. He and Mary
lived and worked in a house in Henley Street. Mary was
from a well-off local family, the Ardens. They'd owned
John's father's farm, so by marrying Mary, John was
moving up in the world.

Shakespeare's birth place,
Stratford-upon-Avon

Elizabethan players performing at an inn in London

At about the time of his marriage, which was probably in 1557, John was elected to the town council. By the time William was born, he'd been appointed **chamberlain**. This was quite an honour. Part of the job was keeping the accounts for the council, and one of his duties was to pay the travelling players who often toured in the summer months to get away from the threat of **plague** in London, 160 kilometres to the south. William would undoubtedly have been taken to see them: it must have been a great treat for everyone when the players came to town.

Brothers and sisters came along: Gilbert in 1566, Joan in 1569, Anne in 1571, Richard in 1574 and finally Edmund, the baby, in 1580. When he was seven, William went to the "petty school", which prepared boys for the grammar school. Only boys went to school – not girls. They had to work hard, but at least they didn't have to worry about spelling: in Elizabethan England, you could spell words exactly how you wanted. Shakespeare's own name could be spelt in lots of different ways: Shaksper, Shackspere, Shaxper ...

After the petty school, William went to the grammar school, where there was just one subject – Latin. No Art, no Geography, no Science – not even Maths or English. But he was introduced to Greek and Roman myths and legends, which he'd later find very useful in his writing.

Shakespeare's school, Stratford-upon-Avon

students being punished at an Elizabethan school

In 1577, the family fortunes took a dive. John owed money – a lot of money. As a result, he lost his position on the council. He'd planned to apply for a **coat-of-arms**, which would mean that he, and his sons after him, would be classified as gentlemen – an honour that he longed for. But now, that was out of the question.

It's not known what William did once he'd left school. He often refers to the law in his plays, so some people think he may have worked as an assistant to a lawyer. Maybe, fascinated by the plays he'd seen, he was already starting to write. His parents must have been mystified; how could he ever hope to earn a living from writing? Didn't he realise he had to help restore the family fortunes and earn some money?

Then, in 1582, when he was 18, William met a girl in a village called Shottery – Anne Hathaway. She was eight years older than him. Her father had been a well-to-do farmer, but when he died, Anne's brother inherited the farm, and now she lived with him and his family – an awkward position for her to be in. She must have been delighted when young William came calling. They married on 28th November, and moved into Henley Street with John and Mary. Their daughter, Susanna, was born the following May. Twins followed in February 1585; they were named Hamnet and Judith, after the Shakespeares' neighbours, the Sadlers.

Anne Hathaway's cottage

12

In 1587, a company of players called the Queen's Men visited Stratford-upon-Avon. Each company had a patron – someone who would help to support them financially. The patron of the Queen's Men was Queen Elizabeth herself, so they must have been pretty good. As usual, everyone flocked to see them – including William.

William was 23, and living in his parents' house with his wife and three small children. Life can't have been easy. Perhaps, as he watched the players, he began to wonder if there was another way – if he could become part of this exciting world, and earn a better living at the same time.

Whatever the reason, in 1587 or soon after, William left Stratford-upon-Avon and went south. His home was still with Anne and his family, but from now on, his work would be in London.

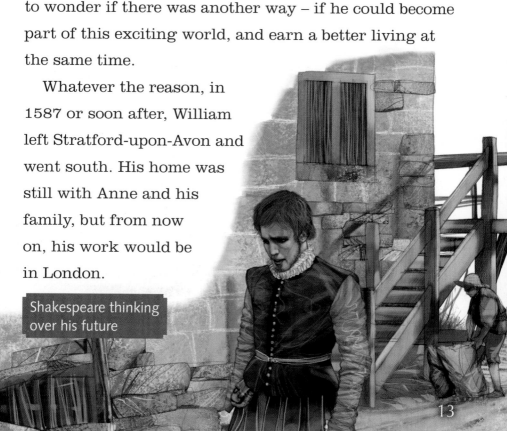

Shakespeare thinking over his future

13

A cross-section of a typical Elizabethan theatre

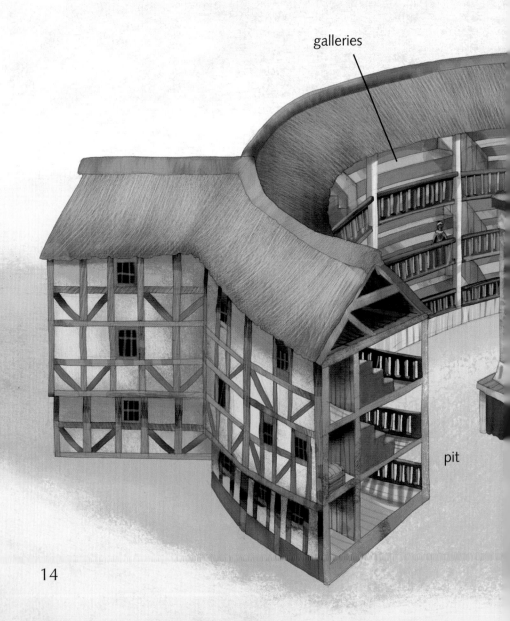

galleries

pit

This gallery above the stage is sometimes used by musicians or as part of the play for example in *Romeo and Juliet*.

upper stage doors

trapdoor

main stage

The big city

London must have been quite a shock to William. There were 1,500 people in Stratford-upon-Avon: in London, there were 200,000. It was busy, crowded, noisy and exciting.

It occupied roughly the area that is now called the City of London. Places like Chelsea and Piccadilly were still peaceful villages out in the countryside. The Thames had only one bridge: mostly people crossed the river by boat. Sometimes a royal barge rowed past, richly decorated in red and gold. You might even catch a glimpse of Queen Elizabeth herself, with her famous red hair – though she was in her fifties now, and the hair was a wig.

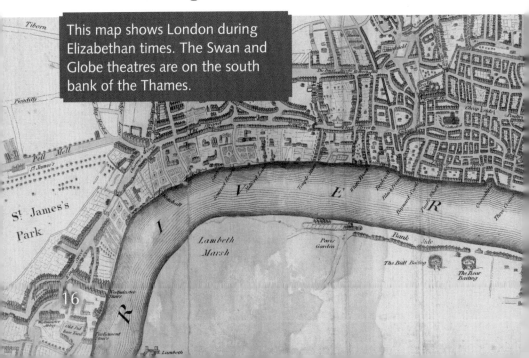

This map shows London during Elizabethan times. The Swan and Globe theatres are on the south bank of the Thames.

Timber-framed houses leant out into narrow streets. Craftsmen worked at open windows to get the best of the light. Music from a **lute** or a virginal – an early kind of piano – might drift out, but it would have to compete with the cries of street traders bringing fresh fruit and vegetables from the countryside, or pedlars with lace, ribbons and pins to sell. And, of course, there was the sound of horses, their hooves striking the cobbles, and market traders shouting to attract customers.

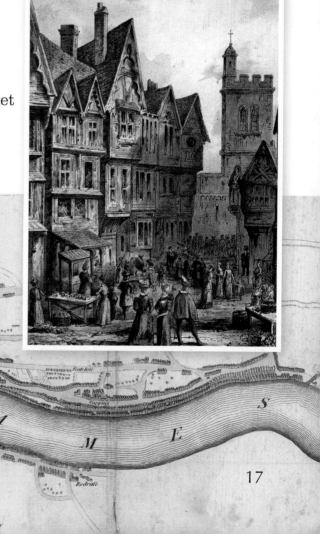

a London street from Elizabethan times

There was a rich variety of smells, too. There was no drainage system, so chamber pots were emptied into the street. There were no baths or showers, and it was quite a business to wash clothes – so if you were in a crowd, you might want to have a little bag of lavender to hold to your nose so you had something sweet to smell. But there were gardens, and birds such as kites that scavenged up the rubbish, and the fruit and vegetables and herbs that people brought in from the countryside freshened the air.

a pomander

The theatres were very popular. Anyone could afford to go: a wealthy noble could pay a shilling (about 12 pounds in today's money) for the very best seat, but a groundling – someone who stood up in the "pit" in front of the stage – need only pay a penny (about one pound now).

When William first arrived, he may have started off working for the "Queen's Men", whom he'd met in Stratford-upon-Avon. (And they *were* all men: there were no women in the company – the women's parts were played by boys.) He probably began by playing small parts, but soon the other players would have noticed that he had a knack for writing. Perhaps he improved a weak speech, or changed an unsatisfactory ending, or put in a few jokes, and when they saw that his alterations worked, they asked him to do more.

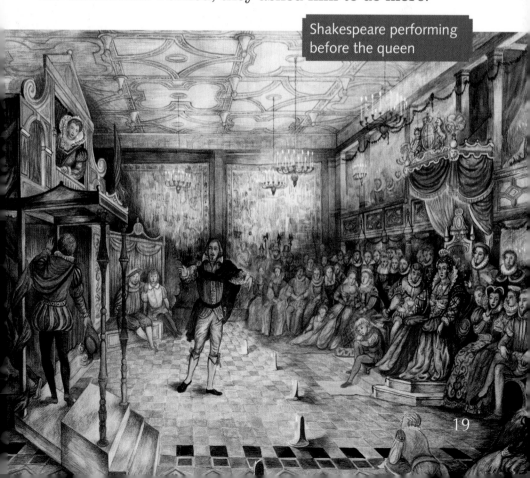

Shakespeare performing before the queen

Certainly by 1592, he was becoming known as a writer. In fact, he was doing so well that other dramatists were starting to get jealous. By this time, William was with Lord Strange's Men at the Rose, a theatre in Southwark, just south of the River Thames. That year, its most successful play was *Harry the Sixth* – now we'd call it *King Henry VI* – and it was listed as being written by a certain William Shakespeare.

It was too much for Robert Greene, an older playwright who had degrees from Oxford and Cambridge and thought he should be a lot more successful than he actually was. And now here was this newcomer, who'd never been to university and had no right at all to be doing so well. Greene watched, and he brooded, and finally he set pen to paper. He wrote an open letter to other scholars, warning them to beware of the players – and of one in particular.

Yes, trust them not: for there is an upstart crow, beautified with our feathers, that with his 'Tiger's heart wrapt in a player's hide' supposes he is as well able to bombast out a blank verse as the best of you, and being an absolute Johannes factotum*, is in his own conceit the only Shake-scene in the country.

* Jack-of-all-trades

Robert Greene in a woodcut from after his death. He is shown wearing his funeral shroud.

Whatever Greene thought of him, the theatre-goers couldn't get enough of Shakespeare's plays, and over the next few years he turned them out one after the other. There were histories about previous rulers of England – the three parts of *Henry VI*, and *Richard III*. There were comedies, including *A Comedy of Errors* and *The Taming of the Shrew*, and there was a very bloodthirsty tragedy called *Titus Andronicus*.

It's difficult to know exactly when they were all written. William's job was to provide a steady stream of hits that would keep the customers coming through the doors; he didn't concern himself with preserving them for the future or getting them accurately printed, and they weren't collected together until 1623, seven years after his death, by his friends and fellow actors, John Heminges and Henry Condell. But, according to the list that's generally agreed, by 1594 he'd written at least seven plays – all of them, remember, in verse!

Shakespeare's plays were not published in book form during his lifetime – he probably wrote them on loose paper.

As well as this, he was also writing poems. In 1592, the theatres were closed because of an outbreak of the plague. William needed to find another way to earn some money. Poetry was popular amongst the **nobility**, and if

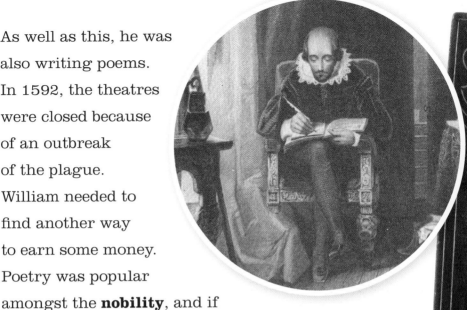

you could find a patron who particularly liked your work, he could be generous with gifts of money. William wrote a couple of long poems on subjects from Roman legends, which he dedicated to the Earl of Southampton, and he also began to write sonnets.

Sonnets are short poems, just 14 lines long, which rhyme in particular places. They are usually about love. William wrote 154 of them over the next few years. One of the most famous sonnets is number 18, which begins:

Shall I compare thee to a summer's day?
Thou art more lovely and more temperate:
Rough winds do shake the darling buds of May …

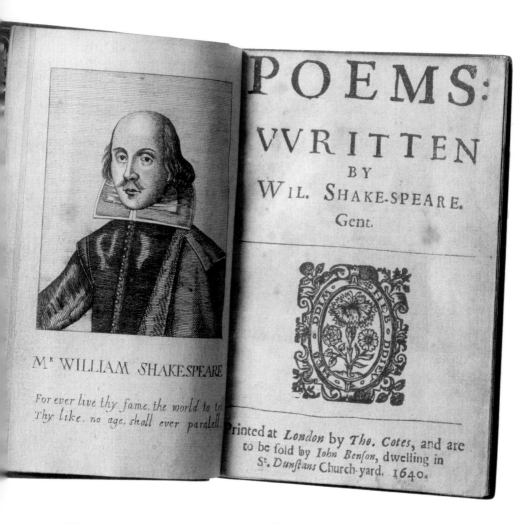

POEMS:
VVRITTEN
BY
WIL. SHAKE-SPEARE.
Gent.

Mr WILLIAM SHAKESPEARE

For ever live thy fame, the world to te[ll]
Thy like, no age, shall ever paralell

Printed at *London* by *Tho. Cotes*, and are
to be sold by *Iohn Benson*, dwelling in
Sᵗ. *Dunstans* Church-yard. 1640.

The poems were popular – *Venus and Adonis*, one
of the longer ones, was reprinted at least nine times
during William's lifetime. And many of the plays were
performed at court, in front of Queen Elizabeth herself.

The newcomer from Stratford-upon-Avon was doing
very well indeed.

Richard III

Richard III is one of what we call "the history plays".
Shakespeare wasn't really bothered about whether
the history was accurate or not. For one thing, his
main concern was to create a play people would
want to watch; for another, Queen Elizabeth I was
the granddaughter of Henry VII, the man who defeated
and killed Richard III in battle – so she wouldn't have
been very pleased if Shakespeare had made Henry out to
be anything other than a hero.

And so Richard is portrayed as an evil monster.
At the beginning of the play, his oldest
brother Edward is the king.
Richard, in the play, has
a hunchback and a bad arm,
and hates the fact that he
isn't handsome and popular,
like Edward. If he could
become king, he thinks,
he'd get his own back on
everyone who had ever
given him a pitying look.

illustration of a battle scene from *Richard III*

Edward is ill, but there are lots of people with a better claim to the throne than Richard: Edward's two sons, his brother Clarence, who comes between Richard and Edward, and Clarence's children. To become king, Richard will have to get rid of all his nephews and of Clarence. So he does – he has them all murdered: he's utterly ruthless. But in the end, Henry Tudor – who actually had only a very shaky claim to the throne – fights Richard at the Battle of Bosworth, kills him, and becomes the first Tudor monarch.

Was Richard really as bad as Shakespeare made him out to be? Sources at the time certainly suggested that he was responsible for the murder of Edward's sons, but nothing was ever proved. However, one fact has recently come to light. In 2012, a skeleton was discovered underneath a car park in Leicester – not far from Bosworth. Scientific evidence has proved beyond reasonable doubt that the body is that of Richard. Although the spine is badly curved, he didn't, in fact, have a hunchback, and wouldn't have been as badly deformed as Shakespeare suggests.

Still – Shakespeare may not have created a historically accurate Richard, but he certainly created one of the lasting villains of all time!

the skeleton discovered underneath the car park in Leicester

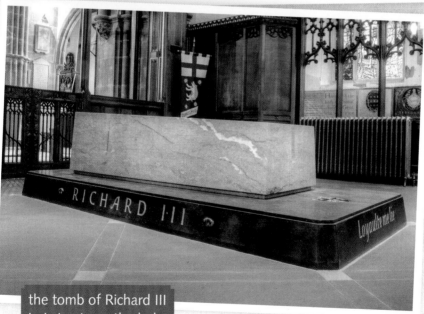

the tomb of Richard III in Leicester cathedral

Success and sadness

In 1594, Lord Strange died. The company soon
found a new patron: Henry Carey, Lord Hunsdon,
the Lord Chamberlain. And so the company became
the Lord Chamberlain's Men. In October 1594, they
moved to The Theatre, in Shoreditch. Soon after
the move, William wrote two comedies – *Two Gentlemen
of Verona* and *Love's Labour's Lost* – and then one
of his most popular plays, the tragedy of *Romeo
and Juliet*, about "a pair of star-crossed lovers" from
feuding families.

The company had its problems, as every players'
company did. The theatres were popular with the people,
but the city leaders didn't like them. Audiences could be
noisy and badly-behaved; if they didn't like a play, they
would shout and throw things at the actors.

But there was also a much more serious problem.
There were outbreaks of the plague most years, and
places where people gathered together helped it to
spread faster; so the theatres were often closed in
the summer. That was a likely time for the players to go
on tour – and perhaps for William to go home and see
his family.

30

But generally, things were going very well for the Lord Chamberlain's Men – and for their star playwright.

However, in 1596, tragedy struck. In August of that year, William's 11-year-old son Hamnet died. There are no surviving letters or diaries – on this, William is silent: there's nothing to tell us in his own words how he felt. But it's not hard to imagine.

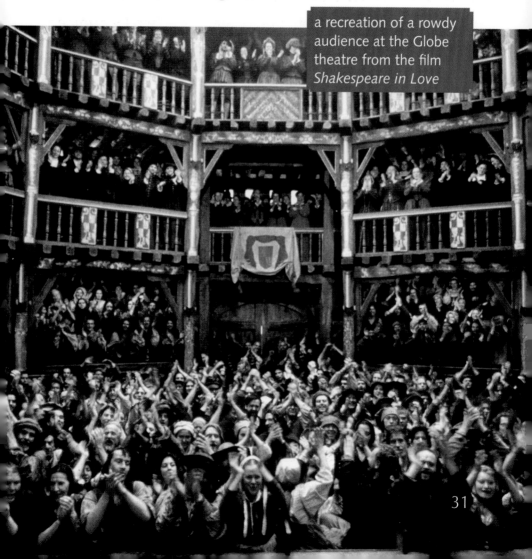

a recreation of a rowdy audience at the Globe theatre from the film *Shakespeare in Love*

It was ironic that this was also the year when the Shakespeares finally got the coat-of-arms that John had first applied for many years before. He'd withdrawn his application then because of his debts and having to leave the council. It was probably granted now because of William's success.

It was meant to give John and his sons the status of gentlemen. But as none of William's brothers had married or had children, Hamnet was the only male heir – and now that he'd died, there was no one to carry on the family name. It must have been a bleak time. In the wider world too, things had taken a darker turn: the Spanish were on the warpath again, and two of England's well-known naval men, Francis Drake and John Hawkins, had been killed.

Sir Francis Drake died in 1596.

But William carried on. What else would he do? He wrote more plays: *King John*, *The Merchant of Venice*, and parts one and two of *Henry IV*. In 1596, he bought New Place, a very fine house in Stratford-upon-Avon. It had been built a hundred years before by Sir Hugh Clopton, who also built the stone bridge which still crosses the River Avon. Like Shakespeare, Sir Hugh had left Stratford-upon-Avon to seek his fortune in London; he'd become the Lord Mayor. Despite the awful sadness of losing his son, William must have felt pleased that he was able to buy such a splendid house for his family, and proud that he was following in the footsteps of such a successful citizen of Stratford-upon-Avon.

the very grand New Place which Shakespeare bought in 1596

Then in 1598, there was a crisis back in London. Giles Alleyn owned the land on which The Theatre stood. When the **lease** came up for renewal, he attached so many conditions to it that Richard and Cuthbert Burbage, the chief **shareholders** in the company, refused to sign. This was exactly what Alleyn wanted: he intended to use The Theatre for another company.

However, there was a clause in the lease which said that the building itself would belong to the Burbages – provided it was removed from the site before the lease ran out. The Burbages had already found another plot of land south of the river, near the Rose. They wanted to build a new theatre, and they wanted to build it fast, in time for the summer season. But where could they get the timber?

transporting The Theatre over the river

The answer was obvious. Over Christmas, while Alleyn was out of London, the Burbages hired a team of workers and went to Shoreditch to tear down the old Theatre. It was so cold that winter that the Thames had frozen over – so it was easy to transport the timber on carts across the ice to the other side of the river.

It worked like a dream. The new theatre was to be called the Globe, and it was to be absolutely splendid. All Giles Alleyn could do was fume.

35

Romeo and Juliet

The play is set in Verona, a town in Italy. It's about two families, the Montagues and the Capulets, who have hated each other for years and are always causing trouble. The prince of Verona has had enough; he announces that the next person to be caught fighting will be put to death. Shakespeare would have seen examples of feuding families all around him. In particular, there were two families, the Danvers and the Longs, who'd been enemies for generations. The two families were always **brawling**, and eventually one of the Longs was killed. The Earl of Southampton, whom William knew well, helped the Danvers brothers to escape to France.

Romeo, the son and heir of the Montagues, decides to gatecrash a masked ball at the Capulet house. There he sees Juliet, the daughter of Lord and Lady Capulet. Before either of them realises who the other is, they fall deeply in love. A friendly priest, Friar Laurence, agrees to marry them in secret the very next day, hoping that the wedding will bring the two families closer together.

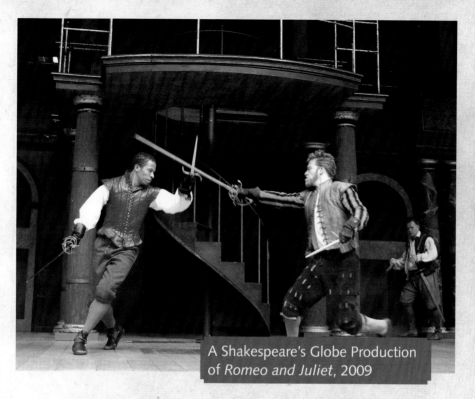

A Shakespeare's Globe Production of *Romeo and Juliet*, 2009

But Tybalt, Juliet's hot-headed cousin, has spotted Romeo at the ball and next day, he challenges him. Romeo doesn't want to fight his new wife's cousin and refuses to be provoked. His best friend Mercutio can't think what's come over Romeo, and says that in that case, he'll fight him. Romeo tries to stop them, but in the struggle, Tybalt kills Mercutio. Full of guilt and grief for his friend, Romeo then kills Tybalt. The prince arrives on the scene, and angrily banishes Romeo from Verona.

After only a few hours with his new wife, he has to leave her – and then her parents declare that she must marry Count Paris. What is she to do?

With Friar Laurence's help, she makes a desperate plan. She'll take a sleeping potion that will make everyone think she's dead. Meanwhile, Friar Laurence will send a message to Romeo and tell him to sneak back and rescue Juliet from the Capulet family tomb.

The messenger is delayed. Believing Juliet to be dead, Romeo buys some poison and rushes back to Verona, determined to kill himself and lie beside her. He finds Paris at the tomb, also grieving for Juliet. They fight, and Paris is killed. Romeo breaks into the tomb, takes the poison and dies. Poor Juliet wakes up and sees what has happened, just as Friar Laurence arrives. She seizes Romeo's dagger and kills herself.

At this point, the families and the prince arrive and Friar Laurence explains what has happened. Horrified at the result of their stupid feud, the families agree to live in peace from now on. The prince has the last word:

> ... *never was a story of more woe*
> *Than this of Juliet and her Romeo.*

Romeo and Juliet continues to be the inspiration for films, ballets and novels to this day. The musical *West Side Story* is a famous example: the story is moved to New York, and instead of the Montagues and the Capulets, the enemies are two rival gangs, the Jets and the Sharks.

A scene from the musical *West Side Story*, 1961

The rise and fall of kings

The 16th century was coming to an end, and so was the long reign of Queen Elizabeth. She'd come to the throne 40 years before in 1558; most of her people had never known another ruler. The prospect of change was worrying – much more so because she refused to decide who was to inherit the throne after her.

All the uncertainty was making people very jumpy. Would the next king be King James the VI of Scotland? He was the son of Elizabeth's cousin, the executed Mary, but he was a Protestant and he'd carefully distanced himself from his troublesome mother. Or perhaps it might be Lady Arabella Stuart, James's cousin, and the great-great-granddaughter of Henry VI? Nobody knew, and Elizabeth wasn't saying.

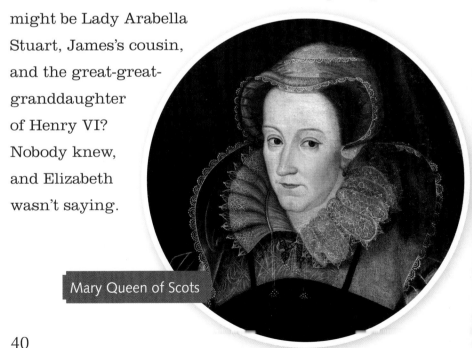

Mary Queen of Scots

There was one person who got tired of all the waiting and wondering and started rebelling against the queen's authority. Robert Devereux, the Earl of Essex, had been a great favourite of Elizabeth. He was a distant cousin, and he was handsome, lively and entertaining.

Unfortunately, he was also hot-headed and arrogant. In 1597, he was sent out to fight the Spanish. The queen had expressly ordered him to tackle the Spanish battle fleet before chasing after their treasure fleet, but he ignored her orders, leaving the English coast almost undefended.

Robert Devereux, The Earl of Essex

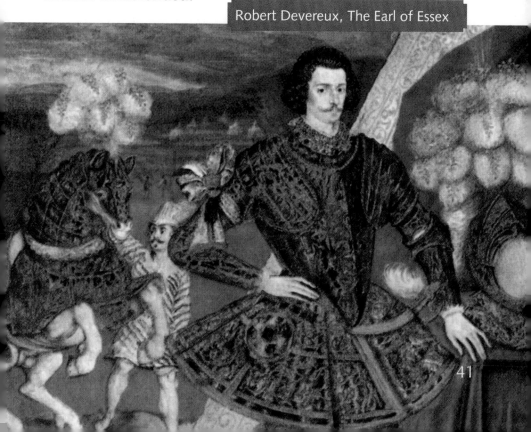

41

She forgave him, and in the following year sent him to Ireland at the head of a great army. But things went badly. Elizabeth angrily ordered him back to London.

Even then, if he had just said he was sorry, all might have been well. Instead, he burst into her private rooms and shouted at her. Everyone was shocked – how dare he do such a thing? He was immediately arrested.

In 1599, William had written a comedy, *Much Ado About Nothing*, and another history play, *Henry V*. His history plays were all about the rise – and the fall – of kings. These might encourage dangerous ideas: if people had got rid of kings in the past, perhaps they could get rid of them in the present, too? The **city fathers** decided it was best to be on the safe side – they didn't want anyone thinking it would be a good idea to get rid of Queen Elizabeth. So they banned plays about anything approaching modern history. Never one for making stories up, William had to go further back to find his subjects, to **Plutarch**'s stories of ancient Rome: he wrote a play about **Julius Caesar**.

The death of Julius Caesar

The company had let its old comic actor (or "fool") go. The new man, Robin Armin, was a very different kind of actor, and William wrote two comedies which would give him the opportunity to show his skills – *As You Like It* and *Twelfth Night*.

Celia, Rosalind and Touchstone from a modern production of *As You Like It*

By 1601, Essex was free again. But his income
had been taken away, and he was out of favour with
the queen. He'd nothing to lose. He made a plan –
and the Lord Chamberlain's Men were to be part
of it. Some of his followers went to the Globe and
asked the players to put on a special performance
of *Richard II*, which William had written several
years earlier. It's a play in which a king is deposed –
forcibly removed from the throne. Essex was making
the point that if it had happened once, it could
happen again. The players were worried, but these were
powerful men, and they didn't feel they could refuse.

The very next day, Essex tried to seize the city.
He failed, and this time nothing could save him: he was
taken to the Tower of London
and executed. Luckily for
the players, although
they were questioned,
they didn't get
into trouble.

illustration of the Earl
of Essex being taken to
the executioner's block

It had all been a bit much, and William didn't write anything else until the autumn. Perhaps the break did him good – because his next play was very different to anything that had been written before. As usual, it was based on an existing story and, once again, it was about the death of kings. But the focus was much more on what the characters were *thinking*, rather than what they were *doing*.

The play was *Hamlet*, and it has fascinated audiences ever since. Even people who think they've never read a word of it will be familiar with some of its most famous lines – especially: "To be or not to be ..."

David Tennant holding the skull of Yorick in a Royal Shakespeare Company production of *Hamlet*

Hamlet

Hamlet introduces a new strain into Shakespeare's writing. Perhaps it reflects the darker mood and uncertainty in the city – or perhaps it reflects his own more serious mood as he grows older and experiences the loss of his son and other family members.

Hamlet, the prince of Denmark, is unhappy. His father has just died and his mother, Gertrude, has already remarried – to Hamlet's uncle, Claudius, who is now king.

On the battlements at night, Hamlet sees his father's ghost. The ghost announces that he was murdered – poisoned by Claudius, his own brother. Hamlet, he declares, must **avenge** him.

Hamlet decides that to distract everyone from his true thoughts and feelings, he'll pretend to be mad. As part of this, he turns against his girlfriend, Ophelia, the daughter of Claudius's chief adviser, Polonius. Meanwhile, he will watch Claudius carefully.

Hamlet feels the ghost's word is not enough; what if it's not really his father's ghost, but a devil sent to

tempt him? It would be wrong to kill Claudius if he's not absolutely certain of his guilt.

Some actors come to court, and Hamlet has an idea. They'll put on a play about a man who murders his brother and marries his sister-in-law:

> The play's the thing
> Wherein I'll catch the conscience of the king.

47

Claudius is clearly rattled and storms out of the performance. Hamlet goes to see his mother and gets very angry with her; he demands to know how she could have betrayed his father by marrying his murderer, Claudius.

Hamlet kills Polonius

Polonius is hiding behind a curtain because he's concerned about Hamlet's state of mind and fears he'll be a danger to the queen. Worried at the way things are going, he shouts for help, at which Hamlet thrusts a dagger through the curtain and kills him. Gertrude is horrified, but Hamlet refuses to say that he's sorry.

Meanwhile, Claudius schemes to send Hamlet to England with his two friends, Rosencrantz and Guildenstern. He gives them a secret letter, ordering the English to put Hamlet to death on arrival. But Hamlet substitutes this letter for one which says that it's Rosencrantz and Guildenstern who must be put to death.

He arrives back in Denmark and is devastated to find that Ophelia, driven mad by his treatment of her and by her father's death, has drowned herself. Her brother Laertes, not unnaturally, blames Hamlet for her death, and he and Claudius make a plan. Laertes will challenge Hamlet to a "friendly" fencing match. This will, in fact, end with Hamlet's death: Laertes' sword will be a real one, not a practice one, and there'll be poison on its point. Claudius, as an extra precaution, prepares a poisoned drink, which he plans to offer to Hamlet.

However, it all goes horribly wrong, and everyone ends up getting killed – Claudius, Gertrude, Laertes, and finally Hamlet himself.

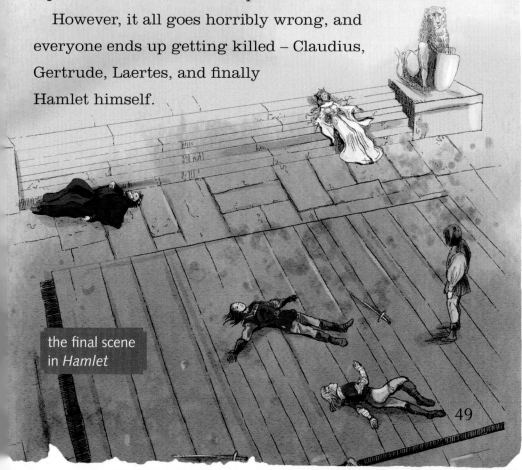

the final scene in *Hamlet*

49

A new century and a new king

In March 1603, the old queen died. If she'd lived another few months, she'd have been 70 – a great age for that time. The leader of her government, Robert Cecil, had for some time been writing secretly to James of Scotland, and he sent messengers to ride at top speed and tell the king to come south. All the plotting to try and get a Catholic on to the throne had come to nothing, and the transfer of power went smoothly.

one of Robert Cecil's messengers

This wasn't the only change for the players. At around the same time, the Lord Chamberlain died, so the company was without a patron. But not for long. Richard Burbage was one of the most famous actors of the day, and William Shakespeare was the best playwright:

Richard Burbage

the king took the company under his own patronage. They were now the King's Men. Also, the king made the senior members of the company – including William – **Grooms of the Bedchamber**. So now the man once described as an "upstart crow" had a position at court: not bad for a country boy from Stratford-upon-Avon!

He had continued to write comedies – *The Merry Wives of Windsor, All's Well That Ends Well* and *Measure for Measure* – and a tragedy based on a tale from Greek mythology, *Troilus and Cressida*. Now, between 1604 and 1606, following on from the success of *Hamlet*, he turned to writing his other three great tragedies: *Othello, King Lear* and *Macbeth*.

It was during this period, in the autumn of 1605, that a very real tragedy almost happened. This was the Gunpowder Plot. If it had succeeded, the king, his parliament, and a lot of the ruling class would have been wiped out in a single terrorist attack. Barrels of gunpowder were smuggled into the cellars below the House of Lords, and the plotters, led by Robert Catesby, intended to set them off at the **State Opening of Parliament**. Their aim was to seize Princess Elizabeth, the king's nine-year-old daughter, install her as a **puppet queen** and restore England to Catholic rule.

Nowadays, people think of the Gunpowder Plot in terms of bonfires and fireworks and fun. But it wouldn't have been much fun for the people of England if the plotters had succeeded. It would have caused chaos and a great many deaths.

The plotters were rounded up, tortured and executed. Before this, James had been quite tolerant; his own wife, Anne of Denmark, was a Catholic, and she'd never pretended to be anything else. But now, Catholics were viewed with great suspicion. Priests were hunted down, and if people continued to practise the old faith, they did so in secret and at risk of their lives.

Guy Fawkes and the Gunpowder Plotters

It was all very different from William's early days in London. James was not as popular as Elizabeth had been. Unlike her, he didn't seem very interested in his subjects. He was passionately fond of hunting, and he spent a huge amount of money on his court, paying for extravagant entertainments called masques. These involved not professional players, but ladies and gentlemen of the court who would dress up in expensive costumes and perform in front of elaborate sets. William didn't write masques, though he does include a short one within *The Tempest*.

In his writing at this time, he was exploring more serious questions: what causes people to become evil? How is it that, through one person's greed or foolishness, a whole country can be plunged into turmoil?

a courtier dressed for a masque

King Lear becomes angry with Cordelia and disowns her

In *Othello*, a great man is brought low by jealousy and by the treachery of a man he trusts as a friend, and as a result, he commits a terrible crime. King Lear's troubles begin when he decides to give up his throne. He listens to the flattering words of his two older daughters, who in fact care only about increasing their own wealth and power, and in the end, leave him with nothing. Cordelia, his youngest daughter, who loves him, is honest with him and doesn't flatter him. In his pride and anger, he turns her away, so that he is left at the mercy of her sisters. In *Macbeth*, the hero is a good man at the beginning of the play, and a monster by its end.

Macbeth

Shakespeare probably chose the subject of *Macbeth*, with its Scottish setting, as a compliment to James. Also, James had a particular interest in witches – in Scotland, he'd supervised the torture and trial of so-called witches, and a few years earlier had written a book about them called *Daemonologie*; *Macbeth* is, of course, famous for its three witches …

the three witches from *Macbeth*

The witches wait on a wild heath for Macbeth, the **Thane** of Glamis, and hero of a recent battle against Norway and two traitors to Scotland – MacDonwald and the Thane of Cawdor. They call Macbeth "Cawdor", which puzzles him, because as far as he knows, Cawdor is still alive. They also predict that Macbeth will become king, and so will the **descendants** of Banquo, the friend who is with him. The witches vanish, and a messenger arrives. He announces that Cawdor has been killed, and that the king, Duncan, has given his title to Macbeth.

Macbeth is shaken. If the witches were right about this, he reasons, could it possibly also be true that he'll become king?

His wife instantly sees that they can make this happen – if they murder Duncan. Macbeth agrees, but then he has second thoughts: Duncan is his king and a good man. Lady Macbeth tells him not to be a coward, and the two of them kill the king and put the blame on his servants. Both their hands are red with blood, but she declares:

A little water clears us of this deed.

Then Macbeth starts to brood on the witches' other prediction – that Banquo's descendants will inherit the throne. What's the point of him committing such a terrible sin just for Banquo's benefit? He decides to have Banquo and his son, Fleance, killed. But Fleance escapes, and later, Macbeth is haunted by Banquo's ghost.

Macbeth's behaviour is spiralling out of control. People are becoming suspicious. He goes to see the witches again, and they make a series of predictions – including that "none of woman born/Shall harm Macbeth", and that he'll never be conquered until "Great Birnam Wood" marches against him. Now Macbeth feels sure he's safe.

News comes that his former friend Macduff has fled to England to seek help from the English against Macbeth. Furious, Macbeth sends men to Macduff's castle to murder his wife and children. Meanwhile, Lady Macbeth is cracking under the strain of all the crimes they've committed. She wanders round the castle, washing her hands over and over again, desperate to wash away the blood that only she can see. As Macbeth's enemies gather to do battle, he's told that his wife has killed herself.

The English soldiers cut off branches from Birnam Wood and advance with them as a shield: the wood itself seems to be moving. Macbeth realises that the witches have tricked him, and that it's all over. He's killed in battle by Macduff. He has been tricked by the witches, but it's his own ambition and greed which have really led to his downfall.

Birnam Wood advancing on Dunsinane Hill

"Our revels now are ended ..."

The celebrated explorers of Elizabeth's reign – men such as Drake, Raleigh and Hawkins – were all dead. But where they'd gone, others dared to follow, even though they knew little of the lands where they hoped to settle. In December 1606, three small ships set off across the Atlantic to **found** Jamestown, the first permanent English settlement in North America. Perhaps their adventure captured Shakespeare's imagination; perhaps he got talking to some of the settlers, or watched the ships setting off. At any rate, five years later he would write *The Tempest*, whose characters inhabit a new world "full of noises/Sounds and sweet airs, that give delight and hurt not."

settlement ships at Jamestown, Virginia, USA

Meanwhile, he wrote another Roman play. This one, *Antony and Cleopatra*, told the story of the famously beautiful Egyptian queen and Mark Antony, who had been Julius Caesar's right-hand man. He followed this up with *Coriolanus*, also set in Rome, and *Timon of Athens* and *Pericles*. These two rather dreary plays are not popular today, and it's probable that Shakespeare co-wrote them with someone else. Perhaps he was tired: perhaps, although he was now a successful playwright and a wealthy businessman with a place at court, he'd had enough of life in London. Perhaps he wished that he, too, could sail away and find a fresh new world.

Richard Burton and Elizabeth Taylor in the film *Cleopatra*, 1963

William began to spend more time in Stratford-upon-Avon. His house, New Place, had orchards and a big garden – so big that he took on a full-time gardener to take care of it. In 1607, his daughter, Susanna, married John Hall, a doctor – a good match – and in 1608, his granddaughter Elizabeth was born. Slowly but surely, the centre of his world was shifting away from London, with its atmosphere of suspicion and fear, and towards his home and his family.

an Elizabethan wedding

In 1610 he wrote *The Winter's Tale*. This is a play that looks as though it's going to be a tragedy, but then changes direction and ends happily. Leontes, like Othello, becomes unreasonably jealous of his wife, Hermione. There's no obvious reason – no evil so-called friend in this play to poison his mind. As a result, he loses his wife, his best friend and both his children. But in the end, he gets all of them except one back again: his family is made whole and his life is renewed. Perhaps it reflects a new-found contentment in Shakespeare's own life.

In this scene from *The Winter's Tale*, Hermione is posing as a statue. Leontes has believed her to be dead for 16 years.

Then, in 1611, came *The Tempest*, the last of his great plays. Again, there's a main character – Prospero – who has a rather hasty temper. But when he has the chance to take revenge on the people who'd injured him years before, he doesn't take it. Instead, he brings them to see what they did wrong, and he forgives them.

Prospero disguises Ariel as a harpy to try to frighten his enemies and bring them to justice

There was one last act to the drama. In 1613, a history play called *Henry VIII* was put on at the Globe. It was probably written partly by Shakespeare and partly by a younger playwright, John Fletcher. At one point in the play, a cannon had to be fired. It should have been an exciting stage effect – but something went wrong. The cannonball lodged in the thatched roof, and a fire began which burnt down the whole theatre.

That was it for Shakespeare. The theatre would be rebuilt, but not by him. This time, he was going home to Stratford-upon-Avon for good.

the New Globe theatre

The Tempest

Prospero is a magician who lives on an enchanted island with his daughter Miranda. The island is inhabited by spirits – notably Caliban and Ariel. By right, Prospero is the Duke of Milan, but he was overthrown 12 years before by his brother Antonio, and Alonso, the King of Naples, who set him and his daughter adrift in a boat.

Prospero discovers that Antonio and Alonso are on a ship close by the island on their way back from a wedding, and he conjures up a storm so that the ship will be wrecked. The crew and passengers make it to the shore in several small groups. Ferdinand, Alonso's son, finds himself alone. He meets Miranda, and the two teenagers fall in love.

Ferdinand telling Miranda he loves her

Meanwhile, two of the sailors meet up with the spirit Caliban, who hates Prospero and persuades them to help him kill the magician. In a parallel plot, Antonio plots with Sebastian, Alonso's brother, to kill Alonso so that Sebastian can become king instead. But Ariel keeps an eye on what everyone's up to and reports back to Prospero, who eventually brings them all together in order to forgive those who have behaved badly and to reconcile them all – even his nasty brother.

Ron Cephas Jones as Caliban in a 2010 production of *The Tempest*

The play was probably written to be part of the celebrations around the wedding of Princess Elizabeth, the daughter of King James I. So there is music, a play-within-a-play, dancing and magical special effects.

Ferdinand and Miranda marry

It's also Shakespeare's last play, and there's a definite sense that, just as Prospero breaks his magic staff and says goodbye to his magic, so Shakespeare is saying goodbye to the stage:

Tim Piggott-Smith as the magician Prospero

Our revels now are ended. These our actors,
As I foretold you, were all spirits and
Are melted into air, into thin air:
And, like the baseless fabric of this vision,
The cloud-capp'd towers, the gorgeous palaces,
The solemn temples, the great globe itself,
Yea, all which it inherit, shall dissolve
And, like this insubstantial pageant faded,
Leave not a rack behind. We are such stuff
As dreams are made of, and our little life
Is rounded with a sleep.

Shakespeare's legacy

Susanna had no more children. William's other daughter, Judith, married just before her father's death. Her husband, Thomas Quiney, was a tavern keeper who had a habit of getting on the wrong side of the law and not paying his debts. William didn't like him at all.

Neither William nor his brothers had a son to carry on the family name. He'd worked so hard, he'd become a gentleman as his father had hoped, he'd achieved so much – and yet the line would end with him.

He died on 23 April 1616. He'd been out with Ben Jonson and Michael Drayton, both fellow playwrights visiting from London, but when he came home he was taken ill. He was 52 – not very old, but still the longest-lived of his brothers. All three of them had died before him: Edmund, the youngest, in 1607, Gilbert in 1611 and Richard in 1612. His sister Joan, who died in 1646 at the age of 77, was the only one to survive into old age. She married a hatter named William Hart, and had four children, one of whom has descendants alive today.

Shakespeare had made a will just a few weeks before, so perhaps he knew he didn't have long to live. He left most of his property to Susanna. Judith was left a small allowance, and there was money in trust for any children she might have. His sister Joan was given the right to remain at the house in Henley Street that

GOOD FREND FOR IESVS SAKE FORBEARE,
TO DICG THE DVST ENCLOASED HEARE.
BLESE BE Y MAN Y SPARES THES STONES,
AND CVRST BE HE Y MOVES MY BONES.

Shakespeare's grave in Stratford-upon-Avon

William had inherited from his father, and he left small bequests to several of his friends.

And what of Anne, his wife? The only thing he left to her was the "second-best bed". People have been very puzzled over this. What did he mean by it? Some people think it shows they were no longer close. Others point out that according to common law, she was owed a third of his estate anyway, and also had the right to stay on at New Place – so Shakespeare knew he didn't need to worry about her future.

But whatever the contents of his will, Shakespeare's real legacy – to all of us – is his work. He wrote about 37 plays, 154 sonnets and five long story poems.

He wasn't the only playwright of his time – far from it. There were others whose work is still performed today – Ben Jonson, for instance, and Christopher Marlowe.

But there's no one else whose plays continue to be performed all over the world, and whose plays have inspired books, films, operas, ballets, music and paintings: no other writer who is so well-known and so well-loved. And this is because although his plays might on the surface be about Tudor kings, or Italian teenagers, or a wizard who lived on an island, they are really about the human heart. They're about what makes us do the things we do, think the things we think, and feel the things we feel.

And of course, he also had a bit of a way with words ...

Glossary

avenge harm a person who has wronged you

brawling fighting in a rough and noisy way – often in the street

chamberlain an important officer of the Town Council, keeping the accounts

city fathers the men responsible for the running of the city of London

coat-of-arms a family crest, mainly for members of the gentry

condemned found guilty of a particular crime and sentenced (often to death)

defiant refusing to obey

descendants the people who come from a particular ancestor

feuding families or groups who dislike each other and go out of their way to pick fights with each other

found set up or create

Grooms of the Bedchamber paid positions at court, which were an honour to hold

Julius Caesar a Roman general and statesman in the 1st century BCE

lease	an agreement to live in or use another person's property in exchange for money
lute	a stringed instrument
nobility	a social class ranked just below royalty
plague	an infectious disease which wiped out millions of people in Europe, also called the Black Death
Plutarch	a Greek historian and biographer
puppet queen	someone on the throne who had the right to be there, but who wouldn't exercise any power, and would be managed by a group of men of the court
shareholders	people who put money into a business, and so own a share of it
State Opening of Parliament	a special ceremony and procession during which the king or queen opens each session of parliament in England
Thane	a man who held land from the king; a term which was used in Anglo-Saxon England, and later on in Scotland

Index

A life's work

1. Stratford-upon-Avon

Shakespeare's birthplace

2. The Big City

Richard III

7. Shakespeare's legacy

37 plays, 154 sonnets and 5 long story poems

3. Success and Sadness

Romeo and Juliet

4. The Rise and Fall of Kings

Hamlet

5. The new century and a new king

The Tempest

The three witches in *Macbeth*

6. Our revels are now ended

 Ideas for reading

Written by Clare Dowdall, PhD
Lecturer and Primary Literacy Consultant

Reading objectives:
- identify and discuss themes and conventions
- summarise the main ideas drawn from more than one paragraph, identifying key details that support the main ideas
- retrieve, record and present information from non-fiction
- explain and discuss their understanding of what they have read, including through formal presentations and debates, maintaining a focus on the topic and using notes where necessary

Spoken language objectives:
- articulate and justify answers, arguments and opinions

Curriculum links: History – British history beyond 1066

Resources: ICT, whiteboards

Build a context for reading

- Ask children what they know about William Shakespeare. Collect information on a whiteboard using a *who, what, where, when, why?* frame.
- Look at the cover and read the blurb. Check children understand the term "playwright".
- Around the outside of the frame, add children's ideas about the time that Shakespeare lived (who ruled, what was life like?)

Understand and apply reading strategies

- Explain that a prologue is an introduction that contains important information and sets the scene.
- Model how to read the first paragraph of the prologue to extract key information and collect words/notes to serve as aide-memoirs.